MATTHEW MCCONAUGHEY, UNDAZED AND UNCONFUSED

Matthew McConaughey, Undazed and Unconfused

All rights about Matthew

McConaughey

Author: Oswald Eakins

DEDICATION

Dedicated to Almighty.

DISCLAIMER

Although the author and publisher have made every effort to ensure that the information in this book was correct at press time, the author and publisher do not assume and hereby disclaim any liability to any party for any loss, damage, or disruption caused by errors or omissions, whether such errors or omissions result from negligence, accident, or any other cause.

Contents

Acknowledgments

Greatly thankful to everyone for their immense
support for the release of this book.

Introduction

Mathew in 2014
Attribution: Avda / www.avda-foto.de

Born on November 4th, 1969, Mathew David McConaughey is one of the most successful Hollywood actors. His first brush with acting was in a 1993 coming-of-age comedy film titled Dazed and Confused. Little did Mathew know that it was the beginning of a trailblazing career that would leave his audience completely floored and a bit "dazed". With his enigmatic smile and rapturous conduct, there is little wonder that Mathew has legions of fan following globally. Dazed and confused was written and directed by Richard Linklater. It had an ensemble cast of actors like Jason London (Randall Floyd), Ben Affleck (Fred O'Bannion), Milla Jovovich (Michelle Burroughs), Cole Hauser (Benny O'Donnell), Parker Posey (Darla Marks), Adam Goldberg, Nickey Katt (Clint Bruno), Joey Lauren Adams, Rory Cochrane(Ron Slater) and Michael playing David Wooderson. The events that happen on the last day of school of some Texas teenagers form the premise of the film. Randall Floyd, played by Jason London, is a promising football player. He has taken a pledge not to consume drugs to not jeopardize the school's chance at the championship. As the classes are ending, the seniors engage on a hunting spree to nail the juniors. Most of them are caught and "paddled". The girls are not spared; they are hazed too. They get beleaguered in the parking lot, get smeared in mustard and raw eggs, and are asked to propose the senior boys. As night approaches, the events take a nasty turn. Set in 1976, the film was a coming-of-age drama, but it was a commercial flop at the time grossing less than 8 million dollars with a production budget of 7 million dollars. Later, the film developed into a cult movie over the years gaining both commercial and critical appreciation ranking third on the list of 50 best high school movies on Entertainment Weekly. The movie garnered the tenth position on the Funniest Movies of the past 25 years' list. Did you know that the title Dazed and Confused was extracted from Jake

Holmes' song? It seems that Linklater had requested to use Rock and Roll song in the film. Apparently, Jimmy Page and John Paul had given their nod, but Robert Plant was recalcitrant.

Mathew's career was taking flight and he acted in several movies in the next twenty years. Contact (1997), Amistad (1997), The Newton Boys (1998), EDtv (1999), U-571 (2000), Frailty (2000) are a few to name. By the turn of the century, Mathew began to appear in rom-com movies like The Wedding Planner (2001), How to Lose a Guy in 10 Days (2003), Failure to Launch (2006), Fool's Gold (2008), and Ghosts of Girlfriends Past (2009). Mathew first appeared in a lead role in 1996 in the movie A Time to Kill, the film adaptation of the eponymous novel by John Grisham. The following year saw Mathew starring opposite legendary actors like Morgan Freeman and Anthony Hopkins in Amistad directed by the acclaimed Steven Spielberg. His movie Contact was sci-fi, the first of its kind in Mathew's career. When Mathew was cast with actresses like Jennifer Garner, Kate Hudson, Sarah Jessica Parker, and Jennifer Lopez, the audience couldn't have enough of it. He simply aced his acting, and the chemistry was natural and affable. Though it established his versatility as an actor, the recurring rom-com movies pigeonholed him as a sex symbol. He desired a break. After a hiatus of two years, Mathew came back to hit the screens in the 2011 film The Lincoln Lawyer movie. By polishing his acting in the legal drama film, Mathew established that he could not only carry romantic, dapper roles but erudite and intellectual roles too. The Lincoln Lawyer was directed by Brad Furman and produced by Sidney Kimmel, Tom Rosenberg, Gary Lucchesi, Richard Wright, and Scott Steindroff. Written by John Romano, the movie saw an array of cast like Marisa Tomei, Ryan Phillippe, Josh Lucas, Michael Pena, etc. Produced with a budget of 40 million dollars, the movie was a commercial success with returns standing at 87 million dollars. Adapted from the 2005 novel, the movie saw Mathew as the titular lawyer. Mathew reinventing himself by experimenting in various genres was named in media as "McConaissance".

A black comedy film Bernie was released in 2011 and in the same year, Mathew starred in Southern Gothic crime Killer Joe for which he received the Saturn Award for Best Actor. The following year Mud was released. Mathew played a supporting role in comedy-drama Magic Mike directed by Steven Soderbergh. The year 2013 was a harbinger of the best career moments for Mathew. He appeared in Dallas Buyers Club, a biographical drama playing Ron Woodroof. His phenomenal performance in the movie brought him much acclaim and the cherry on top- he won the Academy Award for Best Actor, the Golden Globe Award for Best Actor, the Screen Actors Guild Award for Outstanding Performance by a Male Actor in a Leading Role.

The same year, Mathew was seen in The Wolf of

Wall Street directed by Martin Scorsese. Breaking all stereotypes, and daring to tread the least trodden path, Mathew courageously ventured into television when he starred in a crime drama series titled True Detective. In 2014, Mathew was seen in Christopher-Nolan directed Interstellar-the sci-fi film. This role earned him an Emmy nomination for Outstanding Lead Actor in a Drama Series and the Critics' Choice Television Award for Best Actor in a Drama Series.

A Time to Kill (1996)

After kick-starting his Hollywood career in a slew of supporting roles in films like Angels in the Outfield and Texas Chainsaw Massacre, Mathew's breakthrough came in with the legal drama A Time to Kill in 1996. Directed by Joel Schumacher, the film saw Sandra Bullock, Samuel L Jackson, Kevin Spacey, Oliver Platt, and a few other veteran actors. With a budget of 40 million, the film was a commercial success as it garnered 152 million dollars in Box Office. It is a 1996 American crime story based on a novel published in 1989. A Time To Kill was the second novel adaptation of Grisham and directed by Schumacher, the first being The Client. The plot revolves around a crime committed by two local white men Billy Ray Cobb and James Willard who rape an African American ten-year-old Tonya Hailey. After beating her up savagely, the duo hurls her body into a river. Miraculously, Tonya survives the harrowing experience, and the two men are arrested by the Sheriff. Tonya's father, Carl Lee Hailey (played by Samuel L Jackson) seeks the legal aid of a white lawyer Jake Brigance-played by Mathew - who has previously helped in a legal brawl. Brigance tells Carl Lee that the rapists have a good chance at acquittal. Unable to contain his anger and frustration, Carl Lee kills the rapists and accidentally injures a Deputy whose leg is later clinically severed. Consequentially, Carl Lee is incarcerated, and Brigance is ready to defend him. Owing to the racism, rape, and revenge involved, the case has garnered much public attention. The district attorney seeks the death penalty. Matters take a rough turn when the presiding judge Omar Noose denies Brigance's request for a change of venue where there is a more ethnically diverse jury. Eventually, Car Lee's fate is in the hands of an all-white jury. Adding to the grimness is the appearance of the Ku Klux Klan, the white supremacists' gang who are renowned for their pathological hatred for the African American community, the Jews, the leftists, the atheists, etc. However, the battle is not lopsided as counter-protests occur where a motley crowd of blacks, whites who sympathize and support Carl Lee, and other multiracial residents gather to outnumber the Klan members. A nasty brawl ensues, leading to the death of a court official. The Klan tries to hector Brigance to drop the case. When he doesn't back down, the Klan sets his house ablaze. Demoralized and visibly upset, Brigance admits that Carl Lee needn't expect an acquittal. Carl Lee breaks into an emotionally moving monologue and he tells him that despite being sympathetic to him and his ordeal, Brigance was, in the end, a white man and he can only see a black man in Carl Lee. He says that he chose Brigance as his lawyer knowing fully well about his prejudice. He says that Brigance is one of the bad guys and admits that the jury too sees him like Brigance sees him, not just as a man or a father, but as a black man. A visibly shaken Brigance reappears in court and delivers an equally emotionally charged speech exhorting the jury and judge to close their eyes and then hear Car Lee's appeal. Carl Lee had asked Brigance as a white man what it would take to convince him that he was innocent or at least his crime was justified. Fired by the passionate urge to defend Car Lee, Brigance attempts to persuade the jury by expiating and recounting the torture that Tonya endured and after drawing on painful details, he ends his appeal by asking the jury to imagine if Tonya was a white child. The jury is immersed in deliberation. The trepidation was almost palpable. The courtroom was thick with emotionally charged rhetoric from the gathered crowd and jury alike. A heavy pall of tension had descended on the hall. After what seemed like an eternity, a child runs out of the court screaming, "He is innocent".

Who can forget the scene where Brigance in his last-ditch effort at convincing the jury, captivates the audience in a breathtaking acting prowess? He impeccably delivers the lines "killed her tiny womb" and "murdered any chance" for her to have children, his face awash with the unexplainable grief as the character Carl Lee sits ruefully on one corner of the courtroom awaiting his fate that is up in the air. For a minuscule second, we can hear Mathew's voice crack with the weight of the emotions his speech carries. The scene ends with Mathew breaking into tears and the jury equally paralyzed with grief. Some of them are seen wiping their eyes, some are dumb struck at the magnitude of cruelty that now seems unforgivable and unfathomable. With his profoundly moving words, Mathew or Brigance has successfully evoked the brutal image of Tonya, the rape victim, how her tiny body had to bear the ravages of two lecherous, lusty men, how her little beaten body was soaked in their vile semen and her blood, how her battered body and bruised soul was traumatized during the ungodly hours on that fateful day. The moment he delivers "now imagine she is white", the jury is awakened from their dreadful reverie. They have to face the reality; their own prejudices were laid bare. They were called upon to do their bit to deliver a semblance of justice to the man and his family who have been gravely wronged. Mathew's stupendous acting skills ensure that the emotions he intended to deliver surpass the screen and touch every audience watching the scene on the screen. The soul-stirring scene will remain etched in one's memory for a long while after the film ends. The audience is sure to walk out of the cinema with a heavy heart, the imagery Mathew evoked is that strong and impactful. The movie ends with the happy scene where Carl Lee and his family are safe and recovering and a semblance of normalcy returning to their lives after the mind-numbing tragedy had shaken the very foundation of the household. Brigance appears with his wife and daughter and partakes off the merrymaking. Tonya and Brigance's daughter is introduced, and the scene can't be more perfect, both visually and cinematically. The film closes with Carl Lee and Brigance smiling at each other as if a battle in which both had steadfastly fought side by side had come to an end and they had grabbed victory from the jaws of a near calamitous defeat. The movie with its cast of veteran actors playing the lead is still one of the best classic movies of all time. Samuel Jackson, the now-72-year-old maestro is a legend in his own right. He has immortalized Car Lee's character.

Samuel L Jackson

Amistad (1997)

When Amistad was released in 1997, Mathew was only making tentative steps in the industry. It isn't wrong to say that he almost caught the lightning in a bottle when he landed a Steven Spielberg-directed movie in 1997, after only four years of Dazed and Confused and just a year after his first lead role in A Time To Kill.

Written by David Franzoni, Amistad saw an illustrious casting including Morgan Freeman, Anthony Hopkins, Djimon Hounsou, and Mathew McConaughey. Although the movie was a remarkable creation of art and all actors competently performed their parts with equal pizzazz and élan, commercially it grossed just a few million dollars more than the production expense. Thankfully, the worth of an actor or his creation is not measured in the same yardstick as a movies' success at the box office. Mathew received much critical acclaim for his stupendous performance in Amistad, just like Djimon's powerful acting. Based on real events that happened on-board a Spanish ship La Amistad in 1839, the film is a historical drama. The events that occur after Mende tribesmen being transported as slaves manage to take control of their captors form the premise of the film. The legal battle that ensues is resolved by the Supreme Court of United States in 1841. The screenplay by David Franzoni was based on the book Mutiny on the Amistad: The Saga of a Slave Revolt and Its Impact on American Abolition, Law, and diplomacy published in 1987 written by Howard Jones.

The story of La Amistad

La Amistad was a slave ship used to transport slaves from Spanish Cuba to the United States of America in 1839. Joseph Cinque (played by Djimon Hounsou) decides enough is enough and defiantly starts a revolt. The scene where he takes a sword from its shield is impeccably captured by the master director Steven. Djimon's nuanced expression while taking the sword is exemplary of his innate skill as an actor. Emboldened by the support he gathers; Joseph takes over the ship. The mutineers kill the ship crew, sparing two navigators who are commanded to take the ship back to Africa. The embittered navigators foil Joseph's plan by taking the ship to the United States where they are intercepted by the American Navy. The Africans are imprisoned once again as runaway slaves. Captured as slaves in a foreign land and foreign tongue, the Africans find themselves in a quandary. The legal battle charges them of piracy and murder. The Spanish government represented by Martin Van Buren argues that the slaves are its property by some treaty. When two naval officers claim ownership, the two Spanish navigators proffer evidence to show the proof of purchase. Fortunately, the Africans have a lawyer Roger Sherman Baldwin, played by Mathew (Baldwin was an American politician, United States Senator, notable for his 1841 Amistad case) to defend them. Lewis Tappan, an abolitionist had hired Baldwin for the defense. Another black associate of Tappan, Theodore Joadson (Morgan Freeman)-a former slave himself- is also on board. For obvious reasons, Theodore feels the pangs of the captured slaves and he decides to fight for their cause. He defiantly refuses to call them slaves and accords them with the respect of freedom fighters. Baldwin's defense argument is hinged on the idea that the Africans were abducted from a British colony and their trade in America was illegal. Some documents retrieved from the ship helps Baldwin prove his point that the captives belonged to Tecora, a Portuguese slave ship. He argued that the Africans were free citizens. When he notices that the evidence is swaying in favor of the captives, the staff of President Van Buren proposes to replace the presiding judge with a pliant and easily-influenced younger judge.

As the story continues in a gripping narrative, Joseph begins to recount his nightmarish slave life. He was kidnapped by traders outside his village, torn apart from his family, and made to live in a fortress where thousands of slaves lived cheek-by-jowl in abject conditions of squalor and frugality. Eventually, he and thousands of others were sold off to Tecora. The captives were treated as cargo and kept in the brig of the ship. They were frequently beaten, whipped, and sparsely fed. One fine morning, about 50 of them were sent off on a ship that carried them to Havana, Cuba. The captives that were not traded off at an auction were given to La Amistad. The United States attorney tries his best to refute Joseph's claims and questions the veracity of his story, but Royal Navy's Captain Fitzgerald, a passionate crusader of abolition of slavery, corroborates with Joseph's heart-wrenching tale of misery and torture. Baldwin also produces the indubitable proof of Tecora's inventory that evinced clearly that the slave number was reduced by 50, proving Joseph's story and his bona fides. As the legal brawl and counter-arguments draw on, Joseph cries "Give us, us free" in broken English. The judge eventually rules in the favor of Joseph.

Djimon Hounsou in 2016
Attribution: Gage Skidmore

The slave fortress in Lomboko, where the captured

slaves were imprisoned is demolished and its

inmates emancipated. The release of the Africans, however heart-warming to the audience, had ruffled few feathers. The existing resentment and acrimony between the North and the South continue to rankle that eventually leads to Civil War. Joseph got his much-desired freedom and returns home but he never reunites with his lost family. The movie is soul-stirring as it depicts the inordinately long and savagely marred African-American history. The entire film was shot in New England and Puerto Rico. The film begins with the hefty Joseph taking over the Amistad ship in his desperation to attain freedom after years of subjugation and servility. His powerful performance received much acclaim and attention. In the Oprah Winfrey show, where Mathew, Steven Spielberg, and Djimon attended, the audience unanimously gave a standing ovation as Djimon enters the floor. Djimon and Oprah hold each other's hands and stand in silence as the audience's thunderous claps reverberate for a few seconds. It was a moment of deep emotional undercurrents. Oprah and Djimon, both have shared ancestral history. It was a moment observed in reverence and remembrance of the same. Djimon goes on to say how his story is akin to Joseph, the character's story in that he was homeless and was in penury with not enough money to buy food. In a somber voice, he adds that he was on the street like a wayside mendicant for almost a year in Paris. Originally, from West Africa, Djimon was discovered by a fashion designer. Did you know that the character that Morgan Freeman portrays is fictional representing multiple historical personalities?

The Wedding Planner (2001)

The year 2000 turned out to be the harbinger of change for Mathew. After acting in iconic movies under big banners and veteran directors, Mathew was about to begin the journey to becoming a rom-com hero. No matter what movies he did before or after the period of change, the slew of rom-com films he did had made him a household name in the country. Directed by Adam Shankman, The Wedding Planner was written by Michael Ellis and Pamela Falk. With a 35 million budget, the film was a commercial success as it grossed 95 million at the box office. Starring opposite the vivacious Jennifer Lopez, Mathew looked flawless as he aced his role as the charming doctor who falls in love with Jennifer's character Mary who, interestingly, happens to be his wedding planner. Mary has a soaring career as a punctilious wedding planner. She is meticulous, ambitious, and practical. Mary's father wants her to marry her childhood friend Massimo, but she fails to see Massimo as her life partner. Constantly running away from the tangles of marriage, but also desperately searching for her soul mate, Mary meets the genuine and serenely handsome young doctor, Steve Edison (portrayed by Mathew). The couple meets in the most hackneyed manner where the heroine is tripping and the rescuer, the handsome young prince miraculously lands at precisely the same time and place to avert all danger that may have otherwise struck the flawless princess. In the movie, a dumpster comes hurtling at Mary whose shoe gets stuck in a manhole cover. Steve comes to her rescue and saves the day as she-visibly a little dazed and lying on his arms- says in gibberish how Steve smells of peaches and grilled cheese sandwiches. Steve himself is a little smitten with Mary. The meeting was captured on the screen as the quintessential fantasy encounter of hero and heroine, the only problem is Steve was already engaged.

At one dance lesson with one of her clients, Mary is introduced to Fran's (Mary's client) fiancé Eddie who is Steve himself. Fran leaves the two to continue the dance lesson as she is running on some errands. The scene somehow didn't look natural, as it was too contrite. Mary berates Steve for almost kissing her at a previous meeting. Mary is enraged that despite having a fiancé, Steve was encouraging her in a relationship that seemed to have no future. She is in a dilemma because she feels her feelings for Steve will come in the way of the wedding planning and even thinks of quitting. Mary's friend and confidante Penny chides her for wallowing in self-pity and coaxes her to be a professional and get her act together. Her career was paramount, and Penny convinces her to carry on the planning as if nothing had happened. In the meantime, Steve's friend to whom he had confided his feelings for Mary convinces him that it was just a passing fancy owing to the usual "cold feet" just before marriage. The wedding is planned at Napa Valley and on one visit to the potential wedding venue, Massimo decides to show up. To Mary's horror and Steve's shock, he introduces himself to Steve as Mary's fiancé. Steve and Mary have much to talk to each other and settle the confusion and dilemma both faces, but amidst Fran and her overbearing family's presence, they barely get the opportunity to talk. On a horse-riding expedition, Mary's horse goes berserk and Steve, the prince charming comes to Mary's rescue with his male machismo. When intentionally picking a fight with Steve, Mary calls him smug to which Steve takes offense and admonishes her for berating him when she herself was engaged and had kept that fact under wraps.

Upon reaching home, Mary decides to confront her father who keeps pushing her to marry a man she has no interest in whatsoever. Her father, Salvatore confides that his own marriage was arranged, and he found love only months later. This leaves Mary more confused and conflicted. She is gaining a fresher, more practical perspective on marriage. Fran on the other hand seems too engaged with her business trips. She leaves all wedding preparations in the care of Steve and Mary and exits the story briefly. Left to themselves, the two decides to sit and talk things out. Both apologize for each other's previous rudeness and become fast friends. In a very special evening together, Mary pours her heart out, lamenting how her ex-fiancé cheated on her with his college best friend. The magic of the moment is such that she bears her heart and soul letting him know that she is insecure and fears ending up alone and miserable. Steve consoles and comforts her offering his shoulder to cry on. Visibly shaken and moved, Steve decides that Mary needs rest and leaves only to waltz back in to confess his romantic feelings for her. Mary, though equally smitten with the bespectacled, kind pediatrician tells him off saying she can't break Fran's heart. She calls herself a "magnet for unavailable men". It shows her desperation and frustration at being single. It reflects her yearning for companionship.

What follows is almost what one expects. Fran comes back from her trip, approaches Mary, and confides about her own dilemma in marrying Steve. Like an embodiment of righteousness, Mary advises her to go ahead with the wedding, making a stone of her own heart's agonies. In the meantime, Massimo makes a very moving proposal and half-heartedly Mary agrees. Both couples go ahead with their respective weddings, apparently, on the same day. Mary leaves for her wedding handing over Steve-Fran wedding to Penny to handle. One question about their marriage was enough to raise the scepter of doubt in Fran's already flippant mind. Steve asks her in somber notes if they are doing the right thing. Fran immediately realizes the magnitude of the decision and its long-term consequences. Fran calls off the marriage amicably and goes off to her honeymoon alone to indulge herself. Penny takes control of the situation and informs Steve about Mary's decision to marry Massimo.

At the town hall, as Mary and Massimo are about to get married, her father, for the first time sees that his daughter is not happy. This time though it is Mary who is resolutely sticking to her decision to marry Massimo saying that life is not a fairytale and in real life practicality was important rather than the matters of the heart. As she proceeds with the marriage, Massimo saves the day by admitting that he cannot marry her when he knows that her heart belongs to someone else. Finally, the much-hyped and clichéd scenes in most romantic movies happen where the hero is chasing the heroine. The audience is hounded by questions like will they meet, will she say yes, and finally, will they kiss? Although these scenes have been repeated for the umpteenth time on the silver screen, the actors and their impressive acting skills continue to make it look fresh and appealing. The movie made for a perfect fairytale ending when Steve and Mary met and finally, kissed. The sizzling hot romance between Mathew and JLo was phenomenal. The Wedding Planner is one of the films that resulted in Mathew garnering hordes of female fans across the country. Mathew indubitably proved that his acting prowess was not limited to any genre. He can play the erudite lawyer, the geeky guy, and the perfect romantic hero with equal elan.

How to Lose a Guy in 10 Days
(2003)

Directed by Donald Petrie, the film was based on
Michele Alexander and Jeannie Long's book, The
Dos and Don't's of Dating. Mathew was seen
paired against the ravishing beauty Kate Hudson.
Other stars included Adam Goldberg, Michael
Michele, Shalom Harlow and the likes. With a 50
million dollars budget, the film was a stupendous
success commercially garnering a total of 177
million dollars. Andie (played by Kate Hudson) is a
writer. But her job involves writing the "How to"
section for a famous women's magazine,
Composure. She finds her job drab and
meaningless. Andie wants to write on worldly
matters like politics, religion, poverty, which she
thinks is the real kind of problem that needs more
attention. When her friend Michelle played by
Kathryn Hahn is wallowing in yet another break-up,

Andie is encouraged to write an article on "how to lose a guy in 10 days." Andie dates men randomly and has a few tricks up her sleeve to drive them away.

In the meantime, the publicizing chief Benjamin or Ben, played by Mathew is in an attempt to pitch a precious stone mission. When his supervisor attempts to sound him out regarding sentiments, Ben audaciously ventures to say that he can make a woman swoon over him at his whims. Impressed by Ben's pizzazz and confidence, the supervisor accepts his wager and gives him ten days to make a woman fall in love with her. The organizational ball is in the offing and before that, Ben has to accomplish his mission to enamor a woman. Ben's not-so-well-wishing colleagues set him into a trap, asking him to try his charms on Andie knowing fully well that Andie was on a contradicting mission to lose a guy by the same time. Ben and Andie meet, both trying their best to hide their true intentions. In a mission to lose him in less than ten days, to finish her article, Andie does all in her capacity to drive him crazy. Ben on the other hand is desperately clinging to the relationship hoping against all odds to make her fall for him. When Ben is on the verge of breaking up, they attend counseling set up by Michelle. As part of the plan to get things working, Ben and Andie go off to Ben's family in Staten Island. Unlike until now, this weekend retreat will make Andie develop a genuine bond with Ben and she returns to tell her boss that she cannot write the article as she was now genuinely falling for Ben. Her pedantic, bossy boss Lana, played exceptionally well by Bebe Neuwirth, is recalcitrant. In the meantime, Ben takes Andie to his company ball and his boss admits to Ben that he has won in the wager.

Knowing that Ben has won in the bet, his envious co-workers are bent on throwing spanners in the work. Tony (played by Adam Goldberg) and Thayer (played by Thomas Lennon) are falsely informed that Andie knew the bet all along. Worried that

Andie will spoil Ben's success, Tony and Thayer rush to plead with her to keep quiet and play along. Andie, completely unaware of what had been happening is appalled. Ben too learns about Andie's article. The two enter into a verbal spat and part ways. What Ben doesn't realize is that Andie had written in her article how she had lost the only man she loved. If only Ben had read the article, he would have realized that Andie had actually fallen for him. When Ben learns that Andie has quit her job at the Composure magazine and is driving to Washington to attend an interview, he chases her. The two meet and finally confide in each other their true feelings and they kiss.

Did you know that Gwyneth Paltrow was initially thought to play the role of Andie, but she went on to work in View from the Top? The diamond jewelry she flaunts with the gown was real and it is worth millions. For the sake of the iconic "frost yourself" scene alone, 14 million worth of jewelry was loaned. The 80-carat pendant necklace was later auctioned for 5 million. The script received a lukewarm response as it was criticized for being a predictable and "silly" premise. Despite being predictable and clichéd, the film is fun to watch, and Kate comes across as a perky and funny girl who is appalled that she is falling for a man that she is determined to lose in less than ten days. The character of Ben, at times, comes across as a little overbearing, as he is constantly forgiving Andie's clingy and unbearably needy and possessive behaviors. He is a little too confident about his looks and charming personality and mistakenly believes that he can woo any woman at his whims and fancies. The character Ben displays incredible equanimity.

There is an underlying message that the movie seems to deliver. It is the unraveling of the social fabric in our society. Relationships are shallow and disposable. Any number of people gloats over the fact that they have dated umpteen girlfriends/boyfriends in a year. The wedding vows taken on the solemn occasion of marriage have lost their value or are often taken for granted. There is little regard for human emotions and values. Both Ben and Andie have no qualms in going to any extent to deceive each other. Their sole goal is to win in their individualistic career ambitions. Ben's only aim is to win a big diamond account and he is ready to be in a painfully over-bearing relationship with Andie to reach the goal. His mission will end only when he shows off Andie as a prize he won solely with his man-charm and hubris. Ben seems to be completely ignorant about his or his girlfriend's feelings towards each other. Although Ben is unaware of it, he is practicing equanimity. If real-world couples practiced equanimity and tried to work out their differences, this world would have been a far better place and divorce cases would dwindle. Our take away from the movie is to be like the calmest sea, unperturbed and unfazed by the surrounding chaos. Like Ben, let us take a vow to trust that every situation is workable.

Did you know that Mathew almost didn't get cast because the director had scruples in casting him against Kate who was ten years his junior? Kate herself allayed all qualms by saying that she was married to a 36-year old, and Mathew was only 33-year-old at the time; Kate was 23. The rules that Andie uses are extracted from the book that the movie is based on, like talking in a baby voice, calling a man boyfriend immediately after dating, and using the "love" term a little too early. Andie's two best friends are named after the authors of the book. Remember Andie's friends Michelle (Michele Alexander) and Jeannie (Jeannie Long)?

Attribution: David Torcivia
Actor Matthew McConaughey at the 83rd Academy Awards.

Ghosts of Girlfriends Past (2009)

Directed by mark waters, the film was written by
Jon Lucas and Scott Moore. Mathew was cast
opposite the gorgeous Jennifer Garner. Another
one in a slew of myriad rom-com films that
Mathew starred in since the turn of 2000, this is
yet another adaptation of a book A Christmas
Carol, an 1843 novella. The film was shot in Rhode
Island with stars like Emma Stone, Lacey Chabert,
and Michael Douglas. Instead of Christmas eve in
the novella, the film is based on a wedding day and
the previous day. However, the plot remains the
same as in the book. Connor Mead, played by
Mathew is a ladies man, quite a Casanova kind.
While attending his brother's wedding, he bumps
into Jenny Perotti, portrayed by Jenifer Garner, the
only woman he ever loved genuinely. Connor
delivers a speech at the wedding and in an
inebriated state, he sees his uncle Wayne, who had

led an equally promiscuous life. Wayne warns Connor that he will be visited by three ghosts of his ex-girlfriends. They will walk him through his past, present, and future love life. The first ghost is that of Allison, his first love; Emma Stone plays Allison. Alison walks Connor through his relationship with Jenny, how it was all beautiful as a fairytale, and she shows him the exact moment when he fell in love with Jenny. Then after one night of passionate love-making, he does what he does the best-walk out, leaving no trace whatsoever. Connor and Jenny were childhood friends. Connor revisits his childhood moments that he shared with little Jenny where the two are seen sitting on a swing. Connor takes Jenny's picture and promises to keep it forever. Tracing back through such innocent memories makes him question his own behavior. When the two grew up, both were almost in love and it was perfect but for a minor incident where Jenny chose to dance with another boy. It hurt the young Connor and his debauched uncle Wayne advises him never to fall for the trap of romance to avoid getting the stinging pain of lost love or unrequited love. Fired by the advice his "successful" uncle offered him; Connor decides to choose Alison the next time he sees Jenny just to spite her. Years later, the two meet again; the embers of their romance had survived the test of time and the couple decided to give their love a second chance, or was it third?

Jenny exhausts every arrow in her quiver to stop Connor's womanizing ways but in vain. Connor too falls hopelessly in love with Jenny, but he flounders and decides to sneak away while she is still asleep. Jenny wakes up alone and forsaken. She is heartbroken. In the meantime, Connor accidentally knocks down the wedding cake. He is unable to sort it out with Jenny. He realizes that the gathered friends and family are discussing his decadent lifestyle. Paul, his affable brother too opines that Connor should mend his ways. On the other side, he is much peeved that Jenny and Brad are talking privately. Connor's apathy is shunned by all. To make matters worse, Connor accidentally reveals to Sandra, his brother's bride-to-be that years ago Paul has cheated on her. As expected, the wedding is called off, but Connor tries his best to mend the damage. The episode has soured the relationship between Paul and Connor. In between, Ghosts from the Future visit Connor. He sees that Jenny marries Brad, Paul is alone, and the only one to mourn at Connor's funeral was Paul. Wayne reappears to warn him that if his path is not changed, his future is going to be as grim as predicted.

In an attempt to mollify a recalcitrant Sandra, Connor tells her the same advice that he badly needs. The weight of regret at never risking one's heart at all is far greater than the pain of heartbreak. Sandra is convinced, the wedding is back in full swing, and Connor is the photographer of the event. He patches up with Jenny. The picture of little Jenny that he took years ago is still with him and he shows it to her. The two kiss and dance to the same song that Connor had hesitated to dance years before. Wayne vanquishes the Ghost of Girlfriends Future, and everybody is happy once again.

Michael Douglas the veteran actor has done a splendid job acting as Wayne, the promiscuous uncle of Connor. He carries off his part with some aplomb. Breckin Meyer plays Paul and Lacey Chabert is Sandra, Paul's bride-to-be. Reuters had a scathing review about the movie and even went on to mention that the movie will definitely put to test the "drawing power" of both the lead actors, Jennifer and Mathew. The unforgiving article goes on to call the film witless and even launched blistering attacks against the hollowness and repetitiveness of Mathew's roles in rom-com. The writer goes on to opine that the movie is replete with "wince-evoking" sequence. The article disses Mathew's character calling it all too shallow and lackluster. When you read about a sequence in the film where it begins to rain and Wayne tells Connor that its not rain but tears of girlfriends he has cheated or dumped, and how the rain is followed by an avalanche of tissues that were used to soak the tears, which absurdly is followed by a rain of contraceptives that he has used. It is all a little too outlandish to believe that it has all been conceptualized in the film. Garner, for her part, is trying her best but calls it the shoddy script or the shallow story or the lack of it, her character simply fails to convey to the audience as to what she finds attractive in a man who is a habitual offender. In spite of the reviews and the predictions of doom, the movie was a feel-good entertainer, a one-time watch film with much commercial success.

Personal Life

Mathew and Camila Alves in 2010

Mathew met his wife Camila Alves in 2006. The couple has stayed strong ever since. In December 2011, on Christmas eve the couple was engaged. The following year, they married keeping it a very private affair in a catholic ceremony in Austin, Texas. Mathew is a typical Texan man with his strong southern accent and laid-back attitude. It is his very charm and aura. When the most iconic couples like Brad Pitt and Jenifer Aniston split and then a greater shock came when Brad Pitt and Angelina Jolie split, Mathew and his wife have been going strong. With three children; a son in 2008, a daughter in 2010, and another son in 2012, their life seems picture perfect. Though a Christian, he attends a non-denominational church. Did you know that he is planning to run for governor of Texas in 2021? Did you know that he now has you-tube channel?

Mathew started a foundation Just Keep Livin to cater to teenage kids, to help them live meaningful, active lives, and to foster the path to become accomplished men and women. In 2016, he was awarded the Creative Conscience Award for his work and foundation. In 2019, he became the professor of practice at Moody College of

Communication. He has served as a visiting instructor since 2015.

Did you know that the first words he ever said in the film Dazed and Confused were "alright, alright, alright"? His winning Best Actor for the spell-binding performance in Dallas Buyers Club, and the speech he gave on the speech he gave was such a hit that the audience gave him a reverberating and resounding applause. In the movie, Mathew plays the role of a promiscuous Dallas electrician cowboy by the name of Ron Woodroof. Ron is diagnosed with AIDS. His Oscar winning speech had floored the audience and viewers alike. He says how he needs three things everyday- something to look up to, something to look forward to, and someone to chase after. The one he looks up to is God, his family is what he looks forward to, and himself in next ten years-his hero-is what he chases. His hero is always ten years away; he may never become his hero, the chase continues for a lifetime. Mathew is stressing on the importance of having a goal in one's life. Mathew exhorts that everyone of us should have that hero so that we can continue working towards that goal and to that he says "Alright, alright, alright" with some aplomb and flourish holding the memento in his right hand firmly. The audience breaks into uproarious applause and a standing ovation to celebrate the actor and human being that Mathew is.

Conversation with Sadhguru

In a virtual conversation with Sadhguru, a visibly serene Mathew discusses at length a smorgasbord of subjects like fate and destiny, spirituality, karma and success, yoga and religion. His book Green lights published last year. If Mathew is in his air stream in his backyard in Austin, Sadhguru is in the interiors of Georgia. The pandemic has restricted everybody's means to travel but it saves a lot of time and Sadhguru admits that he has done four times more work than ever. Mathew seems to be an avid reader of Sadhguru's books. He seems very keen on karma. The first thing that Mathew talks about is the paradox in our lives and within us. Contradictory to what we believe, he says that that middle ground where the good meets the evil, the truth meets the lies, heaven meets hell is actually not a grey area at all; it is a beautiful space with all the beautiful shades of truth in it. Mathew says that by opening the third eye or the third perspective, we are removing ourselves from the shackles of the limited dual perspective.

Sadhguru widens the scope of the topic by dispelling the myth of contradiction itself. He says that, unlike popular wisdom, truth and lie are not contradictory, life and death are not contradictory, nothing in human life is contradictory, it is our delusion that everything is contradictory. In fact, everything in this universe is complimentary. The only contradictions are only in the psychological space of us humans. Our limited paradigms make us see everything as contradicting. Man and woman are complementary to each other, and not contradicting. If day persisted relentlessly, we would never know what day and night are and vice versa. Human perception is limited. We see only one side of things and it is foolish to believe that only what we see or perceive is present. Realizing the limited perception of our sense organs can widen and deepen our horizon of knowledge.

Fragmented perception creates an illusion of contradictions. Sadhguru expatiates on the profound wisdom and truth of our very existence that despite being a minuscule being on the gargantuan cosmos, each one of us has an individual experience. It is our biggest privilege as human beings to experience individualistic life despite being a cog in the bigger scheme of things. He rues about the fact that people are unaware of the magnanimity of life. We are a universe in ourselves and yet people fail to appreciate it.

The two go on to talk about fate and destiny. Sadhguru differentiates between the two by saying that fate is destiny unattended. If you don't try to forge a path for yourself, if you are lackadaisical in performing your dharma, then things will go in their natural course and only fate awaits you. Fate is not your craftsmanship; it is simply the result of an ongoing process, just an extension of time. When Mathew ponders on how being selfless is a more selfish way to live. Sadhguru once again demolishes the reigning believes and redefines selfishness. He says that there is nothing "self" less in this world. Sadhguru asks his viewers why to be miserly in their selfishness and exhorts people to be "globally selfish". He pulverizes the very concept of selfishness saying that being selfish is ok if it was magnanimous and benevolent selfishness. The problem is people are selfishly hooked onto their idea of religion or country or idea or faith etc.

When Mathew says that he is a fun-loving, quintessential Texan man and how on some serious occasion, his friends admonish him asking him to be serious, Sadhguru breaks into uproarious laughter saying that anybody is allowed to cry only at birth, after that whole life should be about laughing. He says it's almost incongruous to cry other than at birth. Sadhguru goes on to expound that situation in life will never be according to one's wishes. We can try with all our might and skills to make things work in our way, but we should also be mindful that many things are out of our control, and it is a blessing that it is designed like that. When talking about desires coming true, Sadhguru says that no dreams should come true but instead, he wishes that everybody gets things in life that they never even dreamed of. Mathew goes on to talk about chasing the summits in life, reaching the summit only to realize that it was a false summit, or there are several other summits to achieve.

Concerning seeking the treasures of life, Sadhguru makes the viewer realize that life can be about anything, but we can only experience as it is in our minds. No matter what bounty nature offers, nothing matters as long as one's mind is clogged. There can be immense pleasure and pains, but one can experience only one's firmament of mind. He delves into the greatest truth of life that every experience is an inner one. Nothing can be experienced outside of oneself, pain and pleasure, agony and ecstasy, joy and misery. Interestingly, Sadhguru exhorts Mathew and the rest of us to start acknowledging the "I do not know" and that in itself marks the beginning of the greatest mission in life-seeking. Our instinct to seek is stymied by our own ideals, philosophies, ideologies, etc. These prejudices need to be pulverized before seeking the truth in life. this conversation naturally veers to the desert retreat Mathew had taken a few years back. He went out there, in the open, in a foreign land. Initially, he was alone and lost, depressed and under stress, but gradually an inner peace began to seep through his being. His body was getting attuned to the changed situations. He was made to go out of his comfort zone; to go out of the familiar and cozy bubble. Mathew had gone off to Sahara and then to West Texas. Though deeply disturbed and in morass initially, after ten to twelve days, Mathew was in a quest to reinvent himself. Interestingly, his wife was the impetus to go on this journey. The world tells us "I don't know" is a blind spot, but in reality, "I know" is the blind spot.

Sadhguru delves into the very origin and basics of Yoga. He tells us that Yoga was originally meant to yoke. He explains in simple words why the world is today more acrimonious is because there is a constant battle to outdo each other. There is a ceaseless conflict going on between me versus you. For all other species, they are bereft of an individualistic experience. Human beings, on the other hand, are blessed with the privilege of an individualistic experience. If each one of us could experience the whole surrounding as an extension of oneself, the universality of every individual, then there will be at most harmony. In such a state of mind, the very need for morality vanishes. If one is consumed in humanity, morality is not even required. It is when we lose humanity that we need morality. The fundamental meaning of yoga is to yoke oneself to the universality of one's being, to yoke one to that ultimate truth of universality. Just rubbing both hands together for 30 seconds will reveal that there is a force between the two hands when it stops. It is merely because of the sensory expansion. When the sensory body expands to the vastness of the universe, one becomes a yogi.

Mathew delves into landing on the truth for an infinitesimal moment, but when you return to your normal life, how do you retain that truth, that wisdom. Sadhguru redefines maintenance too. he says just like the sky doesn't need maintenance; our spiritual yoking shouldn't need maintenance. Sadhguru reminds us that the means we undertake to get to that level of consciousness is important because consuming drugs or drinks or even activities like sexual indulgences to cross the boundaries of normal perception can be dangerous because such activities can be addictive. He doesn't question the genuineness of these means; he simply says that these activities can get one addicted. To attain a particular state of mind you will be reliant on that particular activity. Sadhguru says that it can be induced by so many means like Native Americans who dance themselves like crazy and attain that psychedelic state- bordering of death and life. Creating an experience within oneself using a drug or drink or activity will make one addicted to that activity or substance.

Extras

Author's Request

Our books are intended to indulge you. If you enjoyed this book or gained any valuable information from it in any way, feel free to share your experience with us. Your contented reviews will help to boost us not only in the sales perspective but also to improve our creativity. Please leave a review at the store front where you purchased this book, and it would be greatly appreciated.

Printed in Great Britain
by Amazon